A is for activist

written and illustrated by

Innosanto Nagara

TRIANGLE
SQUARE

books for young readers

SEVEN STORIES

New York • Oakland

A is for Activist.
Advocate. Abolitionist. Ally.
Actively Answering A call to Action.

Are you an Activist?

B is for Banner, Bobbing in the sky.
Billowing in the Breeze, 'cuz you're not shy!

C is for Co-op.
Cooperating Cultures.
Creative Counter to Corporate vultures.

Oh, and Cats. Can you find the Cats?

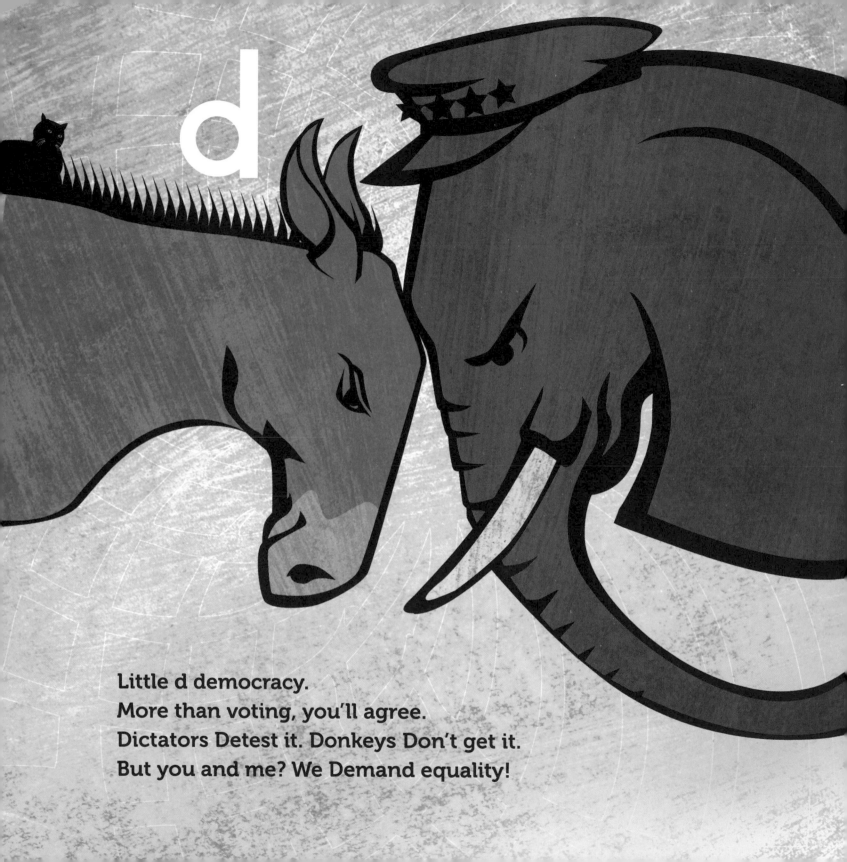

d

Little d democracy.
More than voting, you'll agree.
Dictators Detest it. Donkeys Don't get it.
But you and me? We Demand equality!

Equal rights
Black, brown, or white.
Clean and healthy is a right.
Every place we live and play
Environmental justice is the way!

F is for Feminist.
For Fairness in pay.
For Freedom to Flourish
and choose our own way.

G is for Grassroots.
Sprouting from below.
Sharing nutrients, and the waters' flow.
Below the surface we're all connected.
Stronger together—we Grow.

H is for Healthy food—a Human right.
Honeydew, jicama, nature's delight.
Hummus, Hot dogs, Havarti cheese.
Hot dogs!?!   Yes! Healthy Hot dogs please!
(And pizza.)

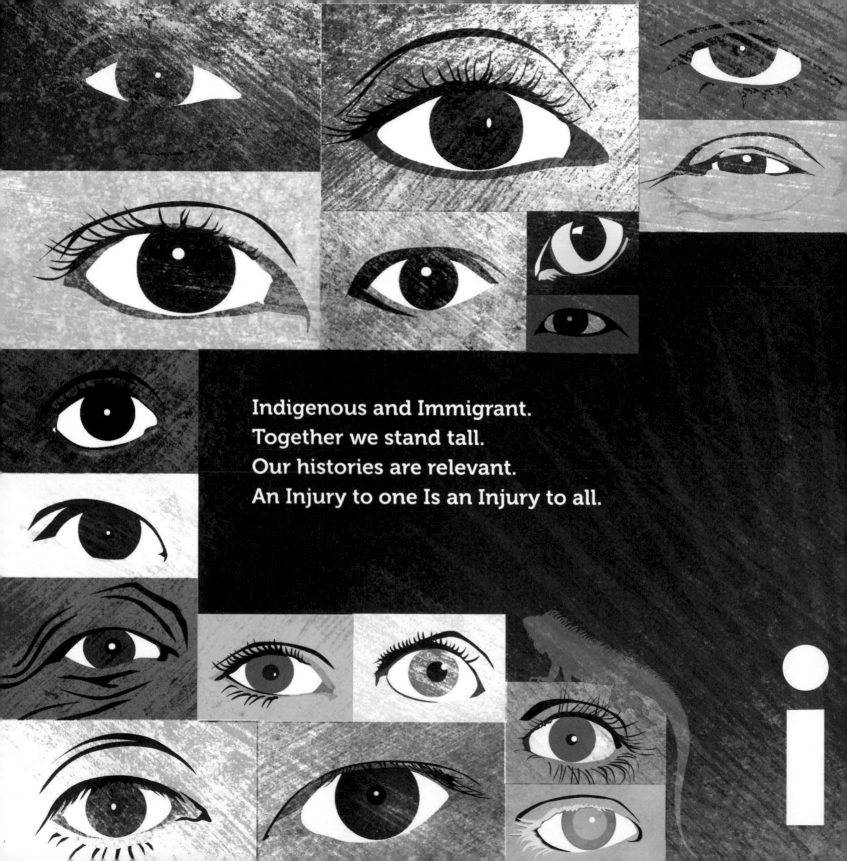

Indigenous and Immigrant.
Together we stand tall.
Our histories are relevant.
An Injury to one Is an Injury to all.

J is for Justice!
Yay for Justice!
Jia-Jing Jiang.
Juanita. Jamal.
Justice for the Janitors,
Justicia for all!

Kings are fine for storytime.
Knights are fun to play.
But when we make decisions
we will choose the people's way!

L-G-B-T-Q!
Love who you choose,
'cuz Love is true!
Liberate your notions of Limited emotions.
Celebrate with pride, our Links of devotion.

Megaphones Marching.
Movimiento Music.
Hip, hip, hooray!
It Must be May Day!

N is for NO.
No! No! No!
Yes to what we want.
No to what must go!
No! No! No!

Open minds Operate best.
Critical thinking Over tests.
Wisdom can't be memorized.
Educate! Agitate! Organize!

Pea-Pea-Peace march!
Pro-Pro-Protest!
Pow-Pow-Power to the Pee-Pee-PEOPLE!
Ya!

Q is for Question.
Questioning coercion.
Querying Qualities counter false assertions.

"Radical Reds!" the headlines said.
"Ruinous Rioters!" the Rumors spread.
"Rabble Rousing Riff Raff . . ."

. . . Really?

S is for Sun, Sol, Solar!
Super Star! Stellar power!
Fuels all life, not just flowers.
Energized homes, cars, and Showers

Silly Selfish Scoundrels Sucking on dinosaur Sludge?
Boo! Hiss!

T is for Trans.
For Trains, Tiaras,
Tulips, Tractors,
And Tigers Too!

Trust in The True,
The he she They That is you!

U is for Weekends.
U is for Workers' Rights!
Wait. That's not U, that's DOUBLE U.
U is for Union. Union yes!!

V is for Vox.
What? Did you say fox?
 No, I said, "Vox."
Did you say box?   No! "Vox!"
Rocks? Blocks? Socks?
"VOX!"
Vox of the people. Voice of the populi.
Better go see the letter D.

Wondrous World.
Wondrous We.
We cannot be Whole
We cannot be free.
Unless we delight
in di-ver-si-ty!

X is for Malcolm.
As in Malcolm X.
History's lessons
can be complex.
Remember Parks.
Remember King.
Remember Malcolm.
And let freedom ring!

Y is for You. And Youth.
Your planet. Your rights.
Your future. Your truth.
Y is for Yes.   Yes! Yes! Yes!

Z is for Zapatista
of course.

Dedicated to Arief Romero
& his mama, Kristi

Text and artwork © 2013 by Innosanto Nagara

A Triangle Square Books for Young Readers Edition, published by Seven Stories Press

Seven Stories Press
140 Watts Street
New York, NY 10013
www.sevenstories.com

Library of Congress Cataloging-in-Publication Data

Nagara, Innosanto.
  A is for activist / Innosanto Nagara.
    pages   cm
ISBN 978-1-60980-539-5 (board)
ISBN 978-1-60980-693-4 (hardcover)
1. Social justice--Juvenile literature. 2. Social activists--Juvenile literature.
3. English language--Alphabet--Pictorial works----Juvenile literature. I. Title.
HM671.N35 2013
303.3'72--dc23
          2013012787

Printed in China

This book was made possible by the generous support and enthusiasm of all those who helped with its creation. Thank you to Design Action Collective, all those who supported the idea on Kickstarter, and all those who pre-ordered and donated to the publication of the first edition.

Thanks to Seven Stories Press and my editor Cory Silverberg for taking A is for Activist to the next level.

Special thanks to Amil, Anna, Eva, Lucia, Miguel, and Sacha (and their parental units) for the expert feedback!

And endless thanks for all the creative help from Kristi Laughlin, Aya de Leon, Jia Ching Chen, Jeff Conant, Lincoln Cushing, Mona Damluji, Gopal Dayaneni, Gerardo Medina, Virali Modi-Parekh, and Miya Yoshitani.